Friedrich Max Müller

Deutsche Liebe

German love

Friedrich Max Müller

Deutsche Liebe

German love

ISBN/EAN: 9783337479404

Hergestellt in Europa, USA, Kanada, Australien, Japan

Cover: Foto ©Thomas Meinert / pixelio.de

Weitere Bücher finden Sie auf **www.hansebooks.com**

Deutsche Liebe

(*GERMAN LOVE*)

Fragments from the Papers of an Alien

COLLECTED BY

F. MAX MÜLLER

TRANSLATED FROM THE SIXTH GERMAN EDITION
By G. A. M.

LONDON
W. SWAN SONNENSCHEIN & CO.
PATERNOSTER SQUARE

1884

PREFACE.

WHO has not once in his life sat down at a desk where shortly before another sat who now rests in the grave? Who has not had to open the locks which for long years hid the most sacred secrets of a heart that now lies hidden in the holy calm of the churchyard? Here are the letters which were so loved by him whom we all loved so well; here are pictures and ribbons and books with marks on every page. Who can now read and decipher them? Who can gather together the faded and broken leaves of this rose, and endow them once more with living fragrance? The flames, which among the Greeks received the body of the departed for fiery destruction,—the flames into which the ancients cast everything that had been most dear to the living,—are still the safest resting-place for such relics. With trembling hesitation the bereaved friend reads the pages which no eye had ever seen, save the one now closed for ever; and when he has satisfied himself by a rapid glance that these pages and letters contain nothing which the world calls important, he throws them hastily on the glowing coals; they flame up, and are gone.

From such flames the following pages were saved. They were intended at first for the friends only of the lost one; but as they have found friends amongst strangers, they may, since so it is to be, wander forth again into the wide world. The Editor would gladly have given more, but the pages were too much torn and destroyed to be collected and pieced together again.

F. MAX MÜLLER.

GERMAN LOVE.

FIRST RECOLLECTION.

CHILDHOOD has its mysteries and its wonders: but who can describe them? who can interpret them? We have all wandered through that silent enchanted forest; we have all, at one time, opened our eyes in a perplexity of happiness, and the fair reality of life overflowed our souls. Then we knew not where we were, or who we were: the whole world then was ours, and we belonged to the whole world. That was an eternal life, without beginning and without end; without break and without pain. Our hearts were bright as the sky in spring, fresh as the scent of the violet, calm and holy as a Sunday morn.

And what disturbs this peace of God in the child? How can this unconscious and innocent life ever have an end? What drives us forth from this bliss of union and communion, and leaves us suddenly alone and desolate in this darkening life?

Say not, with solemn brow, that it is sin. Can a child sin? Say rather that we do not know, and must resign ourselves.

Is it sin that changes the bud into the flower the flower into fruit, and the fruit into dust?

Is it sin that changes the caterpillar into a chrysalis, the chrysalis into a butterfly, and the butterfly into dust?

And is it sin that makes the child a man, and the man hoary-headed, and the hoary head dust? And what is dust? Say rather we do not know, and must resign ourselves.

Yet it is so sweet to look back to the spring-time of life—to gaze into its sanctuary—and to remember. Yes; even in the sultry summer, in the sad autumn, and cold winter of life, there comes now and then a spring day, and the heart says, " I, too, feel as if it were spring." Such a day is to-day, and I lie down on the soft moss in the fragrant forest, and stretch my weary limbs, and gaze upwards through the green leaves into the infinite blue, and think, How was it then in childhood?

All seems forgotten, and the first pages of memory are like an old family Bible,—the opening leaves quite faded, and somewhat crumpled and soiled. Only when we turn further on, and come to the chapters which tell how Adam and Eve were driven out of paradise, it all begins to be clear and legible. Yes, and if we could but find the title-page, with the place and date of the printing! But that is lost, and we only find instead a clean page of writing,—the certificate of our baptism; and there we read, too, when we were born, and what our parents and sponsors were called,—so that we need not think of ourselves as "editions" *sine loco et anno.*

Yes: but the beginning! If there were only no beginning, for with the beginning all thought and memory cease. And when we thus dream back into childhood, and from childhood into eternity, it seems as if the dark beginning always receded, and the thoughts follow, yet never reach it; just as a child seeks the spot where the blue heaven rests on the earth, and runs and runs, and the heaven always recedes before him, yet always rests on the earth; and tne child becomes tired and never reaches it.

But when we once were there—there—here—when we once had our beginning—what do we know then? Memory shakes itself like a poodle who rushes up out of the waves with the water running into its eyes, and most helpless it looks. But I think I can still remember when I first saw the stars. They may have often before seen me; but one evening it seemed to me that it was cold, though I lay in my mother's lap, and I shuddered, and was chilled or afraid,—in short something within me made me more than usually observant of my tiny self. Then my mother showed me the bright stars, and I wondered and thought "how prettily mother has made all that." Then I felt warm again, and probably went to sleep.

Then I remember how I once lay on the grass, and everything round me waved and nodded, and hummed and buzzed. And there came a whole swarm of small, many-footed, winged creatures, and they sat on my forehead and eyes, and said, "Good morning." Then my eyes hurt me, and I called my mother; and she said, "Poor boy, how the midges have stung him." I could not open my eyes, or see the blue sky any more. But my mother had a bunch of fresh violets in her hand, and I felt as if a dark blue, cool fragrance passed through my brain; and even now when I see the first violets I recollect this, and feel as if I must shut my eyes again, that the dark blue sky of those days may rise once more over my soul.

And then I remember how again a new world opened to me; and it was more beautiful than the world of stars and the scent of violets. It was on an Easter morning. My mother woke me early, and before the window stood our old church. It was not beautiful, but it had a high roof, and a lofty tower, and on the tower a golden cross, and it looked far older and greyer than the other houses. Once I had wished to know who lived there; and I looked through the grated iron door. But inside it was quite empty, and cold, and awful,—not one living soul in the whole house; and since then I had always shuddered as I passed by that door. But on this Easter-day it had rained in the early morning, and then the sun had risen in full radiance, and the old church, with its grey slate roof, and the high windows, and the tower with the golden cross, shone with marvellous brightness. Suddenly the light which streamed through the high windows began to wave and seem alive. But it was far too bright to look at; and as I shut my eyes, the light still came into my soul, and everything seemed to shine and be fragrant, and to sing and sound. I felt as if a new life began in me—as if

I had become another being; and when I asked my mother what it was, she said it was an Easter hymn, which they were singing in the church. I have never been able to discover what was the pure holy song which then sank into my soul: it must have been one of those old church songs, such as often broke through the stern soul of our Luther. I have never heard it again. But now, when I hear an adagio of Beethoven, or a psalm of Marcello, or a chorus of Handel,—yes, often, when in the Scotch Highlands or the Tyrol, I hear a simple melody,—I feel as if the lofty church windows were again sparkling, as if the organ notes rang through my soul, and a new world opened, fairer than the world of stars and the fragrance of violets.

This is what I recollect of my earliest childhood, and amidst it floats a loving mother's face, also a father's kind, earnest eyes, and gardens, and a vine-covered arbour, and green soft turf, and a venerable old picture book; and that is all that I can still discern on the first faded pages of memory.

But afterwards it becomes clearer and more distinct. Names and faces stand forth. Not only father and mother, but brothers and sisters, and friends and teachers, and a crowd of strangers. Ah, yes: of those strangers, how much is graven on my memory!

SECOND RECOLLECTION.

NOT far from our house, and opposite the old church with its golden cross, stood a large building, larger even than the church, and with many towers. They too looked very grey and old; but there was no golden cross, only stone eagles were placed on the pinnacles, and a great white and blue flag waved from the highest tower, just over the lofty entrance where the steps went up on each side, and where two mounted soldiers kept guard. The house had many windows, and through the windows could be seen red silk curtains with golden tassels; and all round the court stood the old lime trees, which in summer overshadowed the grey stone walls with their green foliage, and strewed the grass with their fragrant white blossoms. I had often looked up there; and at evening, when the limes smelt sweetly and the windows were lighted up, I saw many forms floating here and there like shadows, and music echoed from the palace above; and carriages drove in, from which men and women stepped out and hastened up the steps. And they all looked so kind and beautiful; and the men had stars on their breasts, and the women had fresh flowers in their hair; and then I often thought, "Why do not you go there also?"

But one day my father took me by the hand and said, "We will go to the palace. You must be very good if the Princess speaks to you, and kiss her hand."

I was about six years old, and rejoiced as one only can rejoice when six years old. I had already had many quiet thoughts about the shadows that I saw in the evenings at the lighted windows; and had at home heard much of the goodness of the Prince and Princess,—how they were so gracious, and brought help and comfort to the poor and suffering, and were chosen by God's mercy to defend the poor and punish the evil-doers. So I had long pictured to myself how everything must go on in the palace; and the Prince and Princess were already old acquaintances, whom I knew as well as I did my nutcracker and my tin soldiers.

My heart beat as I went up the great steps with my father; and while he was still telling me to call the Princess "Your Highness," and the Prince "Serene Highness," the folding doors were opened, and I saw before me a tall figure with bright penetrating eyes. She seemed to come straight towards me, and to reach me her hand. There was an expression on her face which I had long known, and a half-hidden smile played on her cheeks. I could no longer restrain myself; and while my father still stood at the door and (I knew not why) made the deepest bow, my heart seemed to spring into my throat; and I ran to the beautiful lady, and threw my arms round her neck, and kissed her like my mother. The tall lovely lady seemed to be pleased, and stroked my hair and laughed. But my father took me by the hand and drew me away, and said I was very naughty, and he would never bring me there again. My head became quite confused, and the blood flew up into my cheeks, for I felt that my father was unjust to me; and I looked to the Princess that she might defend me; but her face bore an expression of gentle earnestness. Then I looked at the ladies and men who were in the room thinking they would take my part; but when

I looked I saw they were all laughing. Then the tears rose in my eyes, and I ran out through the doorway, down the steps, past the limes in the palace yard, and home, till I found my mother, and threw myself in her arms, sobbing and crying.

"And what has happened to you?" she said.

"Oh, mother!" I cried; "I was with the Princess, and she was such a kind and beautiful lady; so just like you, my dear mother, that I could not help throwing my arms round her and kissing her."

"No!" said my mother. "You should not have done so, for they are strangers, and great people."

"And what then are strangers?" I asked. "May I not love everybody who looks at me with those kind and loving eyes?"

"You may love them, my boy," replied my mother; "but you must not show it."

"Then if it is not wrong for me to love these strangers, why may I not show it?"

Ah, you are right!" she said, "but you must do as your father tells you; and when you are older you will understand why you cannot throw your arms round the neck of every beautiful lady with kind and smiling eyes."

That was a sad day. My father came home, and maintained that I had behaved very badly. In the evening my mother put me to bed, and I said my prayers, but I could not sleep, and kept thinking who those strangers could be, that one might not love.

Alas, poor human heart, even in spring-time thy leaves are blighted, and the feathers torn from thy wings! When the dawn of life unfolds the hidden calyx of the soul, all within is fragrant of love. We learn to stand and walk, to speak and read, but no one teaches us to love; this belongs to us, as our life. Yes: some say it is the deepest root of our being. As the heavenly bodies attract and incline to one another and are held together by the eternal law of gravitation, so heavenly souls lean to and attract one another, and are bound together by the eternal law of love. A flower cannot blossom without sunshine, and a man cannot live without love. Would not the child's heart break from anguish when it feels the first cold blast of this unfriendly world, were it not that the warm sunlight of love shines on him from his parents' eyes, like a softened reflection of heavenly light and love? And the longing which then wakes in the child is the purest, the deepest love: it is a love which embraces the whole world, which flashes up wherever two honest human eyes shine on it, which exults at the sound of a human voice. That is the old immeasurable love,—a deep sea which no plummet has fathomed,—a spring of inexhaustible riches. Those who know it, know too that there is no measure in love,—no increase, no decrease,—but that they who love can only do so with the whole heart, and with the whole soul, with all their power, and with their whole mind.

But, alas, how little remains of this love ere we have passed the half of our life's journey! Even the child learns that there are "strangers," and ceases to be a child. The spring of love is hidden, and, as years go on, is quite choked up: our eyes no longer sparkle, but, serious and wearied, we pass by each other in the noisy streets ; we hardly greet each other, for we know how deeply it wounds the soul when a greeting remains unacknowledged, and how it pains us to part from those whom we have once greeted, and whose hands we have once pressed. The wings of the soul lose nearly all their feathers,—the leaves of the flower are nearly all bruised and withered,—and but a few drops remain of the inexhaustible fountain of love, to cool our tongues, that we may not faint in the desert. These we still call love. But it is no longer the pure, full, joyous love of the child: it is love with doubt and sorrow, burning fire, blazing passion,—love which consumes itself, like rain-drops on hot sand,—love which exacts, not love which spends itself; love which asks, "Will you be mine?" not love which says, "I must be thine:" it is self-absorbed, desperate love. And this is the love which poets sing, and youths and maidens believe in : a fire which flares up and dies down, but never warms, and leaves nothing behind but smoke and ashes. We have all, at some time, believed that these rockets are sunbeams of eternal love. But the brighter the meteor, the darker the night which follows.

And then when all around becomes dark, when we feel utterly lonely, when all men go by us on the right and on the left, without knowing us,—then a forgotten feeling rises at times in the breast, and we know not what it is, for it is neither love nor friendship. "Do you not know me?" we long to cry to every one who passes us so coldly and strangely. Then one feels how man is nearer to man than brother to brother, father to son, friend to friend; and like an old sacred saying, it echoes through the soul, that "strangers" are our nearest and our dearest friends. And why must we pass by them in silence? We know not, and must resign ourselves. Try, when two trains rush past each other on their iron rails, and you see a well-known eye that fain would greet you; try to stretch out your hand, and press the hand of your friend who is flying past you; try it, and you will perhaps understand why man here below passes in silence by his fellow-man.

An old philosopher says, " I saw the fragments of a wrecked ship floating on the sea. Only a few pieces meet and hold together for a little while; then comes a storm and drives them eastward and westward, and they never meet again. So it is with man here below; but no man has seen the great shipwreck."

THIRD RECOLLECTION.

THE clouds on the sky of childhood do not last long, but vanish after a short warm shower of tears. I soon went again to the palace, and the Princess gave me her hand, which I was allowed to kiss; and then she brought me her children—the young Princes and Princesses,—and we played together as if we had known each other for years. Those were happy days, when after school-hours,—for I already went to school,—I might go up to the palace to play. We had all there that heart could desire. Playthings, which my mother had shown me in the shop windows, and of which she told me they were so dear that poor people could live a whole week on the money which they cost,—these I found at the palace ; and, if I asked the Princess, I could take them home to show them to my mother, or even keep them entirely. Beautiful picture-books, which I had seen with my father at the booksellers', but which were only for very good children,—these I could turn over and over at the palace, and study them for hours. And all that belonged to the young Princes belonged to me,—at least I thought so ; for I might not only take away all that I wished, but I often gave the playthings away again to other children : in short I was a young Communist, in the full sense of the word. Only once I remember that the Princess had a golden snake, which clung round her arm as if it were alive, and she gave it us to play with. When I went home I put the snake on my arm, and thought I could frighten my mother well with it. But on the way I met a woman who saw the golden snake, and begged me to show it to her; and then she said, if she might but keep it, she could free her husband from prison. I naturally did not hesitate a moment, but ran away and left the woman alone with the golden snake bracelet. The next day there was a great commotion, and the poor woman was brought to the palace, and cried; and the people said she had stolen the bracelet from me. This made me very angry, and I told them, with earnest zeal, how I had given her the bracelet, and that I did not wish to have it back again. What happened then I do not know; but I remember from that day I showed the Princess everything I took home with me.

It was long, however, before my ideas of *meum* and *tuum* were fully developed; and till a late epoch they melted into one another, just as for a long time I could not distinguish between the colours of red and blue. The last time I remember that my friends laughed at me about this was when my mother gave me some money to buy apples. She gave me a penny, but the apples only cost a half-penny; and when I gave the woman the penny, she said, as I thought in a sad voice, that she had sold nothing the livelong day, and could give me no change: she wished me to buy a penny's-worth. Then I remembered I had also a half-penny in my pocket, and, well pleased that I had solved the difficult problem, I gave it to the woman, saying, "Now you can give me a half-penny." But she understood me so little that she gave me back the penny, and kept the half-penny only.

Now at the time when I went almost daily to play with the young Princes at the palace, and to learn French with them, another form rises to my memory: it was the daughter of the Prince, the

Countess Maria. Her mother died soon after the birth of her child, and the Prince had afterwards married again. I do not remember when I first saw her. She rises slowly and faintly from the twilight of memory,—at first like a shadow of the air, which by degrees takes form more and more, and draws nearer and nearer to me; and at length stands before my soul, like the moon, which on a stormy night suddenly lifts the cloudy veil from her face. She was always sick and suffering and silent; and I have never seen her but stretched on her couch, on which two bearers brought her into our room, and when she was tired carried her out again. There she lay, in her full white drapery, her hands generally folded; and her face was so pale, and yet so sweet and lovely; and her eyes so deep and unfathomable, that I often stood before her lost in thought,—looking at her and asking myself if she too was one of "the strangers." And then she often laid her hand on my head, and I felt as if something ran through my limbs, and I could neither move nor speak, but could only look into those deep, unfathomable eyes. She seldom spoke to us, but her eyes followed our games. However much we romped or made a noise, she never complained, but only held her hands over her white forehead, and shut her eyes, as if asleep. But some days she said she was better; and then she sat upright on her couch; and there was a flush like the early dawn on her cheeks; and she talked to us, and told us wonderful tales. How old she then was I do not know. She was like a child, because she was so helpless; and yet she was so serious and quiet that she could not have been still a child. When people talked of her, they involuntarily spoke softly and low. They called her "the angel," and I never heard anything said of her but what was good and lovable. Often when I saw her lying so helpless and silent, and thought that during her whole life she could never walk, and that there was neither work nor pleasure for her, and that she must always be carried about on her couch till they laid her in her last resting-place, I asked myself why she had been sent into this world, when she might have rested so peacefully in the angels' arms, and they would have carried her through the air on their soft wings, as I had seen in many a sacred picture. Then I felt as if I must take away a part of her suffering, that she might not endure it alone, but I with her. I could not say this to her, for I hardly knew it myself; I only felt, not as if I must fall on her neck,—no one might do that, for that would have hurt her; but as if I could pray from my inmost heart that she might be released from her sufferings.

One warm spring day she was carried into our play-room. She looked very pale, but her eyes were brighter and deeper than ever; and she sat up on her couch, and called us to her. "To-day is my birth-day," she said, "and early this morning I was confirmed. Now, it is possible," she continued, whilst she looked smilingly at her father, "that God may soon call me to Himself,—though I would gladly stay a long time with you. But when I leave you I wish you should not quite forget me, and therefore I have brought a ring for each of you; which you must now wear on your forefinger, and as you grow bigger move it on to the next, till it only fits the little finger, and there you must wear it all your lives."

With these words she took five rings, which she wore on her fingers, and drew them off one by one, and looked so sad and yet so full of love, that I shut my eyes to prevent myself from weeping. She gave the first ring to her eldest brother, and kissed him, and then the second and the third to the two Princesses, and the fourth she gave to the youngest Prince, and kissed each of them, as she gave them the rings. I stood near, looking intently at her white hand, and I saw there was one ring left on her finger, but she leant back and seemed exhausted. Then my eye caught hers, and as a child's eyes speak aloud, she could not but hear what was passing in my thoughts. I had much rather not have had the last ring ; for I felt that I was a stranger, that I did not belong to her, that she did not love me as she did her brothers and sisters. Then I felt a pain at my heart, as if a vein had burst, or a nerve been cut ; and I knew not where to look to hide my distress.

She, however, raised herself up, and laid her hand on my forehead, and looked so searchingly into my eyes, that I felt there was no thought in me which she could not read. Slowly she drew the last ring from her finger, and gave it to me, and said, "I wished to take this ring with me when I leave you ; but it is better that you should wear it, and think of me when I am no longer with you. Read the words which are engraved on the ring : 'As God wills.' You have a wild yet soft heart : may it be tamed by life,—not hardened." And then she kissed me, like her brothers, and gave me the ring.

I can hardly describe what was passing within me. I was then already grown into a boy, and the gentle beauty of the suffering angel had not been without a charm for my young heart. I loved her as a boy can love—and boys love with a fervour, truth, and purity, which few keep in youth and manhood. But I thought she was one of the strangers to whom I might not say I loved them. I scarcely heard the words she spoke to me; I only felt that her soul was as near to mine as two human souls could be. All bitterness was gone from my heart. I felt no longer alone—no longer a stranger, divided from her by a chasm: I was beside her, with her, absorbed within her.

And then I thought it was a sacrifice on her part to give me the last ring, and that she had wished to take it with her to her grave. And a feeling rose up in my soul that overpowered every other feeling, and I said in a trembling voice: "You must keep the ring, if you would give it me; for what is thine is mine." She looked at me for a moment, surprised and thoughtful. Then she took the ring and placed it on her finger, and kissed me again on the forehead, and said softly to me, " You do not know what you say : but learn to understand yourself, and you will be happy, and make many others happy also."

FOURTH RECOLLECTION.

IN each life there are certain years through which we pass as along a dusty poplar avenue, without knowing where we are, and of which nothing remains in the memory but the melancholy feeling that we have been passing on and growing older. So long as the tide of life flows smoothly, it is the same river, only the landscape on either bank seems to change. . But then come the cataracts of life. These remain fixed in the memory, and even when we are far past them, and are advancing nearer and nearer to the deep ocean of eternity, we still seem to hear from afar their roar and tumult,—nay, we feel that the strength of life which remains to us, and drives us onward, has its source and nourishment in those cataracts.

School life was over, and the first merry years of college life were over; and many a fair dream of life was over too. But one thing remained: faith in God and man. Life was very different from what my childish mind had pictured it, yet everything received a higher significance: and what was most incomprehensible and painful was to me the strongest proof of the ever-present hand of God in all earthly affairs. "Not the slightest thing can ever happen to thee, but as God wills it:" that was the short philosophy of life which I had gathered up.

And now I returned in the summer vacation to my small native city. What joy there is in meeting again! No one has explained the cause of it: but seeing again, finding again,—remembering, is the secret of nearly every pleasure and enjoyment. What we see, or hear, or taste for the first time, may be beautiful and pleasant; but it is too new and strange. It surprises us; there is no repose in it, and often the effort of the pleasure is greater than the pleasure itself. But to hear again after many years an old piece of music of which we thought we had forgotten every note, and to recognise it as an old friend; or after long years to stand before the Madonna di San Sisto at Dresden, and allow the feelings to reawaken which the glance into the infinite in the Child's eyes has, in other years, aroused in us; or even to smell a flower or taste a dish of which we have never thought since our schoolboy days;—that gives such deep delight, that we scarcely know whether we rejoice more at the present impression or at the old memories. So, in returning after many years to one's own native city, the soul floats unconsciously in a sea of recollections, and the dancing waves bear it dreamily back along the shores of earlier times. The tower clock strikes, and we feel we shall be too late for school, and then we recover from the fright and rejoice that the fear is over. A dog crosses the street, it is the same dog to whom we always gave a wide berth; now he is old and shows his teeth no more. Here sits an old huckster, whose apples were once a sore temptation, and which, in spite of the dust covering them, we still think must taste better than any apples in the world. There a house has been pulled down, and a new one built. That was the house where our old music-master lived. Oh, how delightful it was to stand here on a summer evening, under the window, and listen how the good old soul amused himself when the hours of the day were over, and improvisé-ed, and like a steam engine, puffing and roaring, let off the superfluous steam accumulated during the day! And here, in this little shady walk—and it then seemed so much larger—here it was, as I came home late one evening, that I met our neighbour's beautiful daughter. Till then I had never ventured to look at her or speak to her, but we boys at school often talked of her, and called her "the beautiful maiden;" and if I saw her at a distance coming along the street, I was so delighted that I could never think of going nearer to her. And here in this little walk, which led to the churchyard, I met her one evening, and she took me by the arm, although we had never then spoken to each other, and said she would go home with me. I believe that the whole way I never spoke one word, nor she either; yet I was so happy that even now, after many years, when I think of it I could wish the time back, and that I could again walk home, silently but happily, with "the beautiful maiden."

And so one recollection rises after another till the waves meet together over our heads, and a sigh rises from our breast, which reminds us that our thoughts have made us forget to take breath. Then at once the dream-world vanishes, like ghosts at the crowing of the cock.

Now when I passed by the old palace and by the lime-trees, and saw the guards on their horses, and the high steps, what recollections rose within me! and how was everything here changed. I had not been to the palace for many a year. The Princess was dead, the Prince had relinquished the government and retired to Italy, and the eldest Prince with whom I grew up had become Regent. He was surrounded by young nobles and officers, whose conversation he enjoyed, and whose society had soon estranged his early play-fellows from him. Other circumstances arose to loosen our former friendship. Like every young man who recognises for the first time the needs in the life of the German people, and the crimes of the German Governments, I had early adopted the views of the Liberal party, and these were as unsuited to a Court as indecorous expressions to a respectable clergyman's family. In short, for many years I had not ascended those steps. And yet in that palace lived a being whose name I pronounced almost daily, and the thought of whom was incessantly present to my mind. I had long accustomed myself to the idea that I should never see her again in this life. She had grown into an image in my mind which I knew did not, and never could exist in reality. She had become my good angel, my other self, to whom I talked instead of talking to myself. How she had become so I could scarcely explain to myself, for I hardly knew her; but as the eye sometimes changes the clouds into shapes, so I felt my imagination had conjured up this lovely vision in the heaven of my childhood, and had formed a perfect picture of the imagination from the faintly traced lines of reality. My thoughts had involuntarily become a dialogue with her; and all that was good in me, all that I strove after, all that I believed in,—my entire better being belonged to her, was dedicated to her, and came from her soul, from the soul of my good angel.

I had barely been a few days in my old house, when one morning I received a letter. It was written in English, and came from the Countess Maria :—

"Dear friend,—I hear you are with us for a short time. We have not met for many years, and if it is agreeable to you, I should like to see an old friend again. You will find me alone this afternoon in the Swiss Cottage. Yours sincerely, MARIA."

I immediately wrote back, also in English, that I would wait upon her that afternoon.

The Swiss Cottage formed a wing of the palace, looking towards the garden, and could be reached without passing through the palace yard. It was five o'clock as I passed through the garden and approached the house. I battled down all my feelings, and prepared for a formal interview. I tried to quiet my good angel within me, and to prove to it that it had nothing to do with this lady; and yet I felt thoroughly uncomfortable, and my good angel would not give me any courage. At length I took heart, muttered something to myself about the masquerade of life, and knocked at the door, which stood half open.

There was no one in the room but a lady, whom I did not know, who also spoke English to me. She said the Countess would be there directly. Then she went away, and I was alone and had time to look about me.

The walls of the room were of oak, and round them ran a trellis-work, on which large broad-leaved ivy climbed over the whole room. The tables and chairs were of oak, and carved. The floor was of inlaid wood. Many old familiar objects were there which I had known in our old play-room in the castle. Other things, and especially the pictures, were new, and yet they were the same pictures which I had in my room at the University. Over the piano hung the portraits of Beethoven, Händel, and Mendelssohn, —exactly the same which I had chosen. In one corner I saw the Venus of Milo, which I always looked on as the most perfect statue of antiquity.

Here on the table lay volumes of Dante, Shakespeare, Tauler's Sermons, the "Theologia Germanica," Rückert's Poems, Tennyson and Burns, Carlyle's "Past and Present!" just the same books which were in my room, and all of which I had but shortly before had in my hands. I began to meditate; but I threw off my thoughts, and was standing before the picture of the late Princess when the door opened, and two bearers (the same I had so often seen as a child) brought the Countess into the room, on her couch.

What a vision! She said nothing, and her face was quiet as a lake, till the bearers had left the room. Then she turned her eyes towards me—the old deep, unfathomable eyes,—and her face brightened every moment, till at last her whole countenance smiled, and she said—

"We are old friends; and I think we have not changed. I cannot say 'you,' and if I may not say 'thou,' in German, we must talk English : do you understand me ?"

I was not prepared for this reception ; but I saw there was no acting here. Here was a soul longing for another soul ; here was a greeting, as when two friends—in spite of their disguises, in spite of their black masks,—know each other by the glance of the eyes. I seized her hand, which she extended to me, and said, " When one speaks to angels, one cannot say ' you.' "

And yet how strange a power lies in the forms and customs of life,—how difficult it is, even with the most congenial soul, to speak the language of the heart. Our conversation flagged, and we both felt the embarrassment of the moment. I broke the silence, and said just what was passing through my mind :

" Men are accustomed from their youth to live in cages ; and even when they are in the free air they dare not move their wings, and are afraid that they may strike against something if they try to fly upwards."

"Yes," she said, "and that is quite right, and cannot be otherwise. We often wish we could live like the birds who fly in the woods, and meet on the branches and sing together, without being introduced to one another. But, my friend, there are owls and sparrows among the birds, and it is good that we can pass them by in life as if we did not know them. It is in life, probably, as in poetry ; and as the real poet knows how to say what is most beautiful and true in a settled form, so men ought to know how to preserve freedom of thought and feeling in spite of the fetters of society."

1 quoted Platen's lines :—

> " What proved itself eternal
> In every age and clime ?

> Unfetter'd thought, though fetter'd
> In chains of words and rhyme."*

"Yes," she said, with a kind and almost arch smile; "but I enjoy a privilege:—my suffering and my loneliness. And I often pity young girls and young men, who can have no friendship and intimacy with one another, but they, or their relations for them, must always think of love, or what people call love. They lose much thereby. Young girls know not what slumbers in their souls, and what might be aroused in them by the earnest conversation of a noble friend; and young men would recover so many knightly virtues, if women could be the distant spectators of the inward struggles of their spirits. But that cannot be; for love always comes into play,—or what is called

---

* " Denn was an allen Orten
  Als ewig sich erweist ?
  Das ist in gebundenen Worten
  Ein ungebundener Geist."

love : quick beatings of the heart, stormy waves of hope, delight in a beautiful face, sweet imaginings, it may be, too, prudent calculations,—in short, all which disturbs that deep ocean-calm which is the true image of pure human love."

Here she suddenly broke off, and an expression of suffering passed across her face. "I must not talk any more to-day," she said : "my doctor will not allow it. I should like to hear a song of Mendelssohn's,—the duet. My young friend could play that many years ago, could he not?"

I could not say anything, for as she ceased speaking, and folded her hands as usual, I saw on her hand a ring. She wore it on the little finger. It was the ring which she had given to me, and I to her. My thoughts were too many for words, and I sat down to the piano and played.

When I had finished, I turned round and looked at her, saying, "If one could only speak thus in music, and without words!"

"We can," she said. "I understood it all, but I can bear no more to-day, for I grow weaker each day. We must become accustomed to one another, and a poor sick hermit may well expect some indulgence. We shall meet to-morrow evening at the same time, shall we not?"

I seized her hand, and would have kissed it; but she held mine tight, and pressed it, saying, "That is best: good-bye."

FIFTH RECOLLECTION.

IT would be hard to say with what thoughts and feelings I returned home. They could not be expressed in words. There are "thoughts without words," which each man plays to himself in moments of great joy and sorrow. I felt neither joy nor sorrow: I felt nothing but inexpressible surprise. Ideas flew across my mind like shooting stars which try to fall from heaven to the earth, but are all extinguished ere they reach their goal. As sometimes in dreams we say to ourselves, "You are dreaming," so I said to myself, "You are awake: it is she." And then I tried to be collected and quiet again, and said to myself, " She is an amiable creature : a very remarkable mind." I even began to pity her. And then I pictured to myself the pleasant evenings I could spend there during the vacation. But no, no: those were not my thoughts. She was all that I had sought for, thought of, hoped and believed in. Here, at length, was a human soul, clear and fresh as a spring morning, fragrant as the violets, bright as the stars. I had perceived at the first glance all that she was, all that was in her: we had welcomed and recognised each other. And my own good angel,—it seemed gone. It answered me no longer, and I soon felt there was but one place in the world where I could find it again.

Now began a bright life. Every evening I was with her, and we soon felt that we really were old friends, and that we could not call each other anything but "thou." It was as if we had always lived by and with one another. There was not a feeling that she touched on that had not already echoed in my soul; and no thought that I expressed but she answered with a kindly nod, as if to say, I thought so too. I had once heard the greatest master of our time improvise with his sister on the pianoforte, and could hardly conceive how two people could so understand each other and feel together, as to give free course to their thoughts, and yet never, even by a single note destroy the harmony of their playing. Now I could comprehend it. Yes: now I first found that my own soul was not so poor and empty as it had always seemed to me, and it was as if the sun alone had been wanting to call to light its buds and flowers. And yet what a sad spring it was that rose over her soul and mine. We forget, in May, that the roses fade so soon; but here, each evening warned us that one leaf after another was falling to the ground. She felt it sooner than I, and spoke of it, without it seeming to give her pain; and our conversations became every day more earnest and solemn.

"I did not think," she said one evening, when I was about to leave her, "that I should live to be so old. When I gave you the ring, on the day of my confirmation, I thought that I must soon take leave of you; and yet I have lived many years, and enjoyed much that was beautiful. I have suffered much too—but one forgets that,—and now, when I feel that the parting is near, each hour, each minute, becomes so precious. Good night: you must not come so late to-morrow."

One day when I entered her room I found an Italian painter with her. She spoke Italian with him, and though he was evidently more of an artisan than an artist, yet she spoke to him with such kindliness, modesty, and even deference, that one perceived at once in her the true nobility of birth, the nobility of soul. When the painter was gone, she said to me, "Now I will show you a picture that will please you: the original is in the Louvre, in Paris. I read a description of it, and had it copied for me by the Italian." She showed me the picture, and waited to hear what I should say. It was the portrait of a man, of middle age, in old German costume. The expression was dreamy and resigned, but yet so true that one could not doubt that the man had once lived. The whole tone of the picture in the foreground was dark and brown; but in the background was a landscape, and on the horizon one perceived the first glimmer of the coming dawn. I could discover nothing in the picture, and yet it had a quieting effect on me, and I could have spent hours with my eyes fixed upon it. "Nothing surpasses a true human countenance," I said, "and even a Raphael could hardly have invented such a one as this."

"True," she said. "But now I will tell you why I wished to have the picture. I read that no one knew the painter, and no one knew whom the picture represented. It is probably a philosopher of the middle ages. I wanted just such a picture for my gallery, for you know that no one knows the author of the "Theologia Germanica," and we have, therefore, no picture of him. I wished to try whether a portrait of an unknown person, by an unknown artist, would do for our German theologian; and if you have nothing to say against it, we will hang it up here, between the 'Albigenses' and the 'Diet of Worms,' and call it the 'German Theologian.'"

"Very well," I said, "but it is rather too powerful and manly for the Frankfort doctor."

"That may be," she answered; "but for a suffering and dying life like mine, there is much comfort and strength to be drawn from his book. I have much to thank him for; for he first brought before me the true secret of Christian doctrine in its wonderful simplicity. I felt I was free to believe or not, for the doctrine of the old teacher, whoever he may have been, had no outward compulsion for me; and yet it seized on me with such power that it seemed as if for the first time I realised what revelation was. And it is just this which closes to so many the entrance into true Christianity,—that its doctrines are brought before us as revelation, before the revelation has taken place within us. This has often disturbed me: not that I have ever doubted the truth and true divinity of our religion, but I thought I had no right to a faith given me by others, and I felt as if that did not really belong to me which I had merely learned and received as a child without understanding it. No one can believe for us any more than they can live and die for us."

"Certainly," I said. "The cause of many heated and violent conflicts lies in this,—that the doctrine of Christ, instead of winning our hearts gradually and irresistibly as it won the hearts of the Apostles and early Christians, meets us from our earliest childhood as the incontrovertible law of a mighty Church, and claims from us an unqualified submission, which we call faith. Doubt will rise sooner or later in the breast of every one who has the power of reflection and veneration for truth, and then whilst we are just in the right way to gain our faith, the spectres of doubt and unbelief rise before us, and hinder the quiet growth of the new life."

"I lately read," she interrupted, "in an English book that truth makes revelation, not revelation truth. And this exactly expresses what I felt in reading the 'Theologia Germanica.' I read the book, and felt the force of its truth so overpoweringly that I was obliged to yield to it. The truth was revealed to me; or rather, I was revealed to myself; I felt for the first time what it means to believe. The truth belonged to me, and had long slumbered within me, but the words of the unknown Teacher pierced through me like a ray of light and illuminated my inward soul, bringing what was dark presentiment into full clearness. And when I had thus once felt how the human soul can believe, I resolved to read the Gospels as if they too had been written by an unknown Teacher. I banished as much as possible the thought that they had been breathed into the Apostles by the Holy Ghost in a miraculous manner—that they had been ratified by Councils, and acknowledged by the Church as the highest authority for the one only saving religion; and then I first learnt to know the meaning of Christian faith and Christian revelation."

"It is only a wonder," I said, "that theologians have not yet deprived us of all religion; and they will do so if the believers do not determinately oppose them, and say to them, 'Thus far, but no further.' Each Church must have its ministers, but there has as yet been no religion in the world which the priests, the Brahmans, the Shamans, the Bonzes, the Lamas, the Pharisees and Scribes have not corrupted and destroyed. They quarrel and argue in a language which is incomprehensible to nine-tenths of their community; and instead of letting themselves be inspired by the Gospel, and inspiring others by the same spirit, they string together long proofs that the Gospels must be true, because they were composed by inspired men. What is this but a poor makeshift for their own unbelief? Whence do they know that these men were inspired in a wonderful manner, without imputing to themselves a far more wonderful inspiration? They evidently felt this themselves, and they therefore extended the gift of inspiration to the Fathers of the Church: they even ascribed it to those who formed the majorities in the determinations of the Councils. But the old question arose again, How do *we* know that among fifty Bishops twenty-six were inspired and twenty-four not? Then comes at length the last despairing step; and we are told that by the laying on of hands inspiration and infallibility dwell in the head or heads of the Church even to this day, and that the infallibility of these men, utter strangers to us, makes all inward conviction, all self-surrender, all faithful introspection superfluous. But for all that and all that, the old, simple question will never be silenced—How can B know that A is inspired, unless B be as much inspired as A, or even more? for to know that A is inspired does surely involve more than being inspired oneself."

"I had not so clearly comprehended this," she said; "but I often felt how difficult it must be to know if any one truly loves, for there is no sign of love that may not be falsified. And then I thought that no one could know it but he who himself knows what love is, and that he also would only believe in the love of another so far as he has faith in his own love. And as with the gift of love, so it is with the gift of the Holy Ghost—those on whom it descends hear a sound from heaven as of a mighty wind, and see the cloven tongues as if they were of fire; but the others are terrified, and become angry, or mock and say we are 'full of new wine.'

"But, as I told you, it is the 'Theologia Germanica' that I have to thank for teaching me to believe in my faith, and just what to many would seem a defect, strengthened me the most—namely, that the old Teacher never thinks of regularly proving his propositions. He scatters them as a sower, in the hope that some seeds will fall on good ground, and bear fruit a thousand fold. So also our Divine Teacher never sought to prove His doctrines, for the full consciousness of truth disdains the form of demonstration."

"Yes," I interrupted her, for I could not help

thinking of the wonderful chain of demonstration in Spinoza's Ethics; "and therefore the scrupulous care with which Spinoza produces his arguments always gives me the impression that this acute reasoner could not have believed his own doctrines with all his heart, and had, for that very reason, felt the need of fastening so strongly each mesh of the net. But," I continued, "I must own I do not share this great admiration for the 'Theologia Germanica,' though I have to thank the book for many suggestions. But to me it is wanting in the human and the poetical, and above all, in a warm feeling and reverence for the real. The whole Mysticism of the fourteenth century seems to me useful as a preparation; but it first attained its solution in that manly and courageous return to actual life which we find in Luther. Man must, once in his life, perceive nothingness; he must feel that of himself he is nothing; that his being, his beginning, his eternal life, are rooted and hid in something superterrestrial and incomprehensible. That is the return to God which in this life, indeed, never leads to the goal; but it leaves a divine longing after home which never ceases. But man cannot abolish the act of creation as the Mystics desire. Though formed from nothing, that is to say, by and of God alone, he cannot through his own power return to nothing; and the self-annihilation of which Tauler so often speaks is hardly better than the Nirvâna, or the 'going out' of the human soul, of the Buddhists. Tauler says 'that if, from great reverence and love to the Highest, he could become a nothing, he would willingly sink before God's Majesty down to the lowest abyss.' But this annihilation of the creature was not the will of the Creator, for He created it. 'God makes Himself into man,' says Augustine, 'not man into God.' Mysticism should only be as the ordeal by fire, to steel the human soul, not to dissolve it away into vapour like boiling water in a cauldron. He who has perceived the nothingness of Self should yet recognise this Self as a reflex of the truly divine Self. The 'Theologia Germanica' says:

"'That which has flowed forth from the Perfect is no true substance, and hath no substance except in the Perfect, but is an accident or a brightness, or a visible appearance, which is no substance and hath no substance, except in the fire whence the brightness flows forth, such as in the sun or a candle.'

"But that which flows from the Divine Being, be it but as the flame of the fire, must yet have Divine reality in itself, and one might almost ask, What were the fire without flame, the sun without light, the Creator without the creature? But these are questions of which it is truly said:

"'Whatever man or creature desireth to dive into and understand the sacred counsel and will of God desireth the same as Adam and the devil.'

"Therefore it should be enough for us to feel that we are a reflex of the Divine Being, and to shine more and more unto the perfect day. The divine light which is in us we may not place under a bushel or extinguish, but let it shine forth to lighten and warm all around us. Then we feel a living fire in every vein, and a higher consecration to the battle of life. Even the smallest duties remind us of God : the earthly becomes divine, the temporal eternal, and our whole life is as a life in God. God is not eternal rest, but eternal life, and this Angelius Silesius forgets when he says, 'God is without will.'

*' We pray, O Lord our God, do Thou Thy holy will! And see, God has no will : He is at peace and still.'"

---

* Wir beten, "Es gescheh' mein Herr und Gott dein Wille," Und, sich, er hat nicht Will; er ist ein' ew'ge Stille.

F

She listened to me quietly, and after a little reflection said, "Health and strength are required for your faith, but there are also life-weary souls who long for rest and sleep, who feel themselves so lonely, that when they fall asleep in God they will miss the world as little as the world will miss them. To them it is a foretaste of heavenly rest when they can even here lose themselves in the Divine; and they can do so because no bond binds them to this world, no wish disturbs their heart but the desire for rest.

* ' Rest is the highest good, and were our God not rest,
   I must needs close my eyes, though by His vision
      blest.'

"And you are unjust to the German theologian. He teaches, indeed, the nothingness of

---

* Ruh' ist das höchste Gut, und wäre Gott nicht Ruh,
Ich schlüge vor ihm selbst meine Augen beide zu.

outward life, but he would not therefore see it annihilated. Read me the 28th Chapter."

I took the book and read, whilst she shut her eyes and listened.

"'Now when this union truly cometh to pass and becometh real, the inward man standeth henceforward immovable in this union; and God suffereth the outward man to be moved hither and thither, from this to that, among such things as are necessary and right. So that the outward man saith in all sincerity, " I have no will to be or not to be, to live or die, to know or not to know, to do or to leave undone, and the like; but I am ready for all such things as are necessary and right, and obedient thereunto, whether I have to do or to suffer." And thus the outward man has no wherefore or purpose, but only to satisfy the Eternal will. For it is perceived of a truth, that the inward man shall stand immovable, and that it is needful for the outer man to be moved. And if the inward man have any *Wherefore* in his movements, it is only that such things must be, and ought to be, as are ordained by the Eternal will. And where God Himself is the Man, it is thus, as we plainly see, in Christ. Moreover, where all this takes place in and from a divine light, there is no spiritual pride or irreverent freedom, but boundless humility and a lowly, broken heart; also an honest, blameless walk, justice, truth, peace, content, and all that is of virtue must needs be there. Where it is otherwise, there it is wrong, as we have said. For just as neither this thing nor that can bring about or further this union, so there is nothing which hath power to frustrate or hinder it, save the man himself with his self-will, that doeth him this great wrong. Of this be well assured.'"

"That is enough," she said; "and I think we understand each other now. In another place our unknown friend says yet more plainly, that no man can be still before death, and that the Godlike man is like the hand of God, and does nothing of himself but what God wills, or is like a house in which God dwells. And a man filled with God's Spirit feels this indeed, but does not speak of it, but guards his life in God like a secret of love. I often feel like that silver poplar before my window. Now in the evening it is quite still, not a leaf trembles or moves, and even when the morning air stirs and shakes every leaf, still the stem with its branches stands firm and immovable; and when the autumn comes, every leaf, once so full of life, falls to the ground and decays;—but the stem awaits another spring."

She had learnt to live so entirely in this world that I did not wish to rouse her from it. Had I not torn myself from the magic circle of these thoughts with great difficulty? and I hardly knew whether she had not chosen the good part which could not be taken from her, whilst the rest of us are careful and troubled about many things.

So each evening brought a fresh conversation, and with each evening a new vista opened itself to me into this immeasurable mind. She had no secret from me; her conversation was merely thinking and feeling aloud; and all that she said must have lived in her for many years, for she flung out her thoughts as carelessly as a child, who having picked its lap full of flowers throws them away on the grass. I could not open my soul to her so freely as she opened hers, and that oppressed and disturbed me. And yet amidst the ceaseless untruths which society imposes on us, call them custom, politeness, discretion, prudence, worldly wisdom, or anything else, how few can retain or recover, even when they wish it, the full truth of their nature! How few remember that they are but wearing a mask in life's masquerade! Even love may not speak its own words, or keep its own silence, but must learn the jargon of the poets; and must rave and sigh, instead of freely greeting, and gazing, and giving itself away. I would rather have confessed to her, and said, "You do not know me;" but I felt my words were not entirely true. Before I went away I left with her a volume of Arnold's poems, which I had just received, and begged her to read one called "The Buried Life." This was my confession; and then I knelt by her couch, and said, "Good night." "Good night," she said, and laid her hand on my head. And again something stole through all my limbs, and the dreams of childhood floated through my spirit, and I could not move, but I looked into those deep, unfathomable eyes, until the peace of her spirit overshadowed my own. Then I rose and went home silently; and in the night I dreamed of a silver poplar, round which the wind roared, but not a single leaf in its branches moved or trembled.

THE BURIED LIFE.

Light flows our war of mocking words, and yet.
Behold, with tears mine eyes are wet

I feel a nameless sadness o'er me roll.
Yes, yes, we know that we can jest,
We know, we know that we can smile!
But there's a something in this breast
To which thy light words bring no rest,
And thy gay smiles no anodyne.
Give me thy hand, and hush awhile,
And turn those limpid eyes on mine,
And let me read there, love, thy inmost soul!

Alas, is even love too weak
To unlock the heart, and let it speak?
Are even lovers powerless to reveal
To one another what indeed they feel?
I knew the mass of men conceal'd
Their thoughts, for fear that if reveal'd
They would by other men be met
With blank indifference, or with blame reproved;
I knew they lived and moved
Trick'd in disguises, alien to the rest
Of men, and alien to themselves!—and yet
The same heart beats in every human breast.

But we, my love,—doth a like spell benumb
Our hearts?—our voices?—must we too be dumb?

Ah! well for us, if even we,
Even for a moment, can get free
Our heart, and have our lips unchain'd;
For that which seals them hath been deep ordain'd!

Fate, which foresaw
How frivolous a baby man would be,
By what distractions he would be possess'd,
How he would pour himself in every strife,
And well-nigh change his own identity;
That it might keep from his capricious play
His genuine self, and force him to obey
Even in his own despite his being's law,
Bade through the deep recesses of our breast
The unregarded river of our life
Pursue with indiscernible flow its way;
And that we should not see
The buried stream, and seem to be
Eddying at large in blind uncertainty,
Though driving on with it eternally.
But often, in the world's most crowded streets,
But often, in the din of strife,
There rises an unspeakable desire
After the knowledge of our buried life,
A thirst to spend our fire and restless force
In tracking out our true, original course;

A longing to inquire
Into the mystery of this heart that beats
So wild, so deep in us,—to know
Whence our thoughts come and where they go.
And many a man in his own breast then delves,
But deep enough, alas, none ever mines!
And we have been on many thousand lines,
And we have shown, on each, spirit and power;
But hardly have we, for one little hour,
Been on our own line, have we been ourselves!
Hardly had skill to utter one of all
The nameless feelings that course through our breast:
But they course on for ever unexpress'd!
And long we try in vain to speak and act
Our hidden self, and what we say and do
Is eloquent, is well—but 'tis not true,
And then we will no more be rack'd
With inward striving, and demand
Of all the thousand nothings of the hour
Their stupefying power;
Ah yes, and they benumb us at our call!
Yet still, from time to time, vague and forlorn,
From the soul's subterranean depth upborne
As from an infinitely distant land,
Come airs, and floating echoes, and convey
A melancholy into all our day.

Only, but this is rare!
When a belovèd hand is laid in ours,
When, jaded with the rush and glare
Of the interminable hours,
Our eyes can in another's eyes read clear,
When our world-deafen'd ear
Is by the tones of a loved voice caress'd,—
A bolt is shot back somewhere in our breast.
And a lost pulse of feeling stirs again.
The eye sinks inward, and the heart lies plain,
And what we mean, we say, and what we would, we know!
A man becomes aware of his life's flow,
And hears its winding murmur, and he sees.
The meadows where it glides, the sun, the breeze.

And there arrives a lull in the hot race,
Wherein he doth for ever chase
That flying and elusive shadow, rest.
An air of coolness plays upon his face,
And an unwonted calm pervades his breast.
And then he thinks he knows
The hills where his life rose,
And the sea where it goes.

SIXTH RECOLLECTION.

EARLY the next morning there was a knock at my door, and my old doctor entered. He was the friend, the guardian of every soul and body in our little city. He had seen two generations grow up, and the children that he had brought into the world had themselves become fathers and mothers, and he looked upon them all as his own children. He was unmarried, though even in his old age he might still be called strong and handsome. I never knew him otherwise than as he then stood before me: his clear blue eyes shining from beneath his bushy eyebrows; his white hair, still full of youthful vigour, curling and thick. I see his shoes with silver buckles, his white stockings, and the brown coat, which always looked new, and yet always seemed the old one; and his gold-headed cane was the same which as a child I had often seen standing by my bed-side when he felt my pulse and prescribed medicine for me. I had often been ill, but faith in this man always made me well again. I never had the least doubt that he could cure me; and when my mother said she must send for the old doctor to make me well again, it was the same to me as if she had said she must send to the tailor to mend my torn trowsers : I had only to take the medicine, and I felt that I must recover.

"How are you, my young friend?" he said, as he entered the room. "You do not look quite well,—you must not study too much. But I have no time to-day for talking : I only came to say, you must not go again to the Countess Maria.

I have been with her the whole night, and that is your fault; therefore, mind, if her life is dear to you, do not visit her again. As soon as possible she must go away into the country. It would be better if you were to travel for a while. So good day, and be a good boy."

With these words he gave me his hand, looked kindly into my eyes as if he would exact a promise from me; and then went on further to visit his sick children.

I was so astonished that another person should all at once have penetrated so deeply into the secrets of my soul as to know what I myself hardly knew, that I only began to think when he was already far up the street. Then my heart began to heave like water that has long stood beside the fire without movement and suddenly boils up, and bubbles, and mounts, and hisses, till it overflows.

Not to see her again? I only live when I am near her. I will be quiet; I will not speak a word to her; I will only stand at the window as she sleeps and dreams. But not to see her again? Not even to take leave of her? She does not know,—she cannot know, that I love her. I do not love her. I desire nothing; I hope nothing: my heart never beats more quietly than when I am near her. But I must feel her presence; I must breathe her spirit; I must go to her: and she expects me. And has fate brought us together without intention? Am I not to be her comfort? Is she not to be my rest? Life is no mere game: it does not drive two human souls together like two grains of sand in the desert, which the simoom whirls together and then drives apart. The souls which are brought near us by a kind fate, we must hold fast, for they are intended for us, and no power can tear them from us if we have courage to live, to struggle, to die for them. She would despise me if I were to give up her love at the first clap of thunder, like the shadow of a tree beneath which I had dreamed away so many happy hours.

Then suddenly all became still within me, and I heard only the words, "her love," and they sounded again from every corner of my heart as an echo, and I was frightened at myself. "Her love,"—and how had I deserved it? She hardly knew me, and if she could ever love me, must I not myself confess to her that I did not deserve the love of an angel? Each thought, each hope that rose in my soul fell back, like a bird which tries to soar into the blue sky and does not see the wire which incloses him on every side. But then, wherefore all this blessedness so near, and so unattainable? Cannot God work miracles? Does He not work miracles every morning?

Has He not often listened to my prayer, when it rose to Him in full faith and would not let Him go till it won comfort and help for the weary? It is no earthly blessing for which we pray; it is only that two souls who have found and recognised each other may finish this short journey of life arm in arm, face to face,—that I may be a support to her in her sufferings, and she my comfort or my sweet charge till we reach the goal. And if a late spring were still granted to her life, if her sufferings were removed,—oh, what blessed pictures passed before my eyes! The castle of her mother in the Tyrol belonged to her. There, on the green hills, in the fresh mountain air, among a healthy unspoiled people, far away from the bustle of the world, from its cares and struggles, with no one to envy us, no one to judge, in what blessed peace we could contemplate the evening of life, and " silently pass away like the evening glow." Then I saw the dark lake, with the glance of its living waves, and in them the clear reflection of the distant glacier; and I heard the bells of the herds, and the songs of the herdsmen, and saw the hunters with their rifles clamber over the mountains, and the old and young gather together of an evening in the village,—and over all I saw her form floating like an angel of peace, and I was her guide and her friend. "Fool," I cried aloud: "fool, is thy heart still so wild and so weak? Nerve thyself: think who thou art, and how far removed from her. She is kindly, and she likes to see herself mirrored in another soul; but her childlike confidence and ease best prove that no deeper feeling for thee lives in her breast. Hast thou not seen on many a bright summer night, in wandering alone through the beech woods, how the moon shed its silver light over every branch and leaf, and how it even lighted up the dark, gloomy waters of the fish-pond, and reflected itself brightly in the smallest drop? So she looks out upon this night of life, and thou mayest bear her soft light reflected in the heart, but hope not for a warmer ray."

Then her image rose suddenly, as if alive, before my eyes! she stood before me, not as a memory, but as a vision, and for the first time I was aware how beautiful she was. It was not the beauty of form, or of colouring, such as dazzles us at the first sight of a lovely maiden, and which will pass away as quickly as a spring blossom. It was the harmony of her whole being, the truth of every movement, the spiritual expression, the perfect interpenetration of body and soul, which gave such delight to those who saw her. The beauty which nature lavishes so profusely does not please, unless the possessor can appropriate it, and, as it were, deserve and conquer it. No: it rather offends; as when we see an actress on the stage advance in royal robes, and observe at every step how little her dress suits her, how little it belongs to her. Grace is real beauty, and grace alone is the spiritualizing of all that is dull and material and earthly; it is that presence of the spirit which can even make the ugly beautiful. The more closely I observed the vision which stood before me, the more I perceived the noble beauty of every lineament, and the depth of soul that lay in her whole being. Oh, what blessedness was near me! and was it all only to show me the highest summit of earthly happiness, and then to cast me down for ever into the flat sandy waste of life? Oh, that I had never imagined what treasures this earth holds! But to love once, and then to be alone for ever! to believe once, and then to despair for ever! to see the light once, and then to be blind for ever! that is torture compared to which all human torture-chambers are as nothing.

And thus the wild hunt of my thoughts swept on and on till at last all became still, and the whirling feelings were gradually collected and composed. Men call this quiet exhaustion reflection; but we are really not reflecting, we are only looking on. We leave our thoughts to themselves till they shoot into crystals spontaneously, or according to eternal laws; we watch the process like an attentive chemist, and when the elements have taken their form we often wonder that they and we are so very different from what we expected.

The first word I spoke as I roused myself from my trance, was, "I must go." I sat down that same moment and wrote to the doctor that I was going away for a fortnight, and left all to him. An excuse was soon found for my parents, and that evening I was on my way to the Tyrol.

SEVENTH RECOLLECTION.

TO wander arm in arm with a friend through the valleys and over the mountains of the Tyrol, gives us fresh strength and joy of life ; but to pursue the same way alone with one's thoughts, is but lost time, lost toil. Of what benefit to me are the green mountains, and the dark ravines, the blue lake, and the mighty waterfall? Instead of my looking at them, they look at me, and wonder at the desolate human face ; and it almost broke my heart to feel that I had found no one in the whole world who would rather be with me than with any other human being. With such thoughts I woke every morning, and, like a tune that we cannot get out of our heads, they followed me the whole day. And when of an evening I entered the inns and sat down wearily, and the people in the room looked at me, and every one wondered at the lonely wanderer, my feelings often forced me out again into the night, when no one saw me alone; and then I crept back again, quite late and went softly up to my room, and threw myself on my hot bed, and till I slept, that song of Schubert's echoed through my soul: "Peace is where thou thyself art not." At length the sight of the people, that I met everywhere rejoicing and glad and laughing amid the exquisite scenery, became so insupportable that I slept during the day-time, and pursued my journey from place to place during the clear moonlight nights. There was, at least, one feeling that drove away and diverted my thoughts, and that was fear. For let any one try to climb up the mountains alone the whole night through, on an unknown road, when the eye unnaturally strained sees distant forms which it cannot distinguish, when the ear with morbid intensity hears sounds without knowing whence they proceed, when the foot suddenly stumbles, be it over a root breaking through the rock, or over a slippery path moistened by the spray of a waterfall,—and at the same time a hopeless blank in the heart,—no recollections by which to warm the soul, no hope to which to cling; let any one try this, and both outwardly and inwardly he will feel the cold chill of night. The earliest fear of the human heart arises from being forsaken by God; but life drives this away, and men, all children of God, comfort us in our loneliness. But when their help and love forsake us again, then we feel what is meant by being deserted by God and man, and nature with its dumb glance frightens us more than it consoles us. Yes, even when we plant our foot firmly on the solid rocks, they seem to tremble like the foam of the sea from whence they once slowly arose; and when the eye longs for light, and the moon rises behind the fir woods and draws their sharp points on the bright wall of rocks opposite, they look to us like the dead hands of a clock which was once wound up, and will some day cease to move. Even in the stars and the distant vault of heaven there is no support for the soul, which trembles and feels itself alone and deserted. Only one thought brings us comfort sometimes ;—that is, the quiet, the order, the immensity, and the certainty of Nature's work. Here, where the waterfall has clothed the grey stone on both sides with dark green moss, deep in the cool shadow a blue forget-me-not suddenly catches the eye : it is one of millions of sisters that now bloom by every streamlet and over every meadow of the earth, and have bloomed ever since the first morning of creation scattered the whole wealth of inexhaustible power over the world. Each line on its leaves, every stamen in its calyx, every filament of its roots is numbered, and no power on earth can increase or decrease them. When we aid our dim-sighted eyes, and with superhuman power look deeper into the secrets of nature, when the microscope opens to us the quiet laboratories of the seed, of the buds, and of the flowers, we perceive anew in the finest tissues and cells the same constantly recurring form, and in the slightest filaments the eternal unchangeableness of nature's laws. Could we go still deeper, the same world of forms would everywhere meet our eyes, and as in a room surrounded with mirrors, the eye would lose itself in endless repetitions. Such an infinity lies buried in this little flower; and if we look up to heaven we trace the same eternal order, as moons revolve round planets, planets round suns, and suns round new suns; and to the sharpened eye the most distant nebula becomes a beautiful new world. Think then, how those majestic stars circle round and round that the seasons of the year may change, that the seed of this forget-me-not may rise again into life, the cells open, the leaves spring forth, and the flowers adorn the carpet of the fields; and think of the butterfly that cradles itself in the blue cup of the flower, and whose awakening to life, and whose enjoyment of existence, whose living breath is a thousand times more wonderful than the tissues of the plant, or the dead mechanism of the heavenly bodies, and feel that thou also dost belong to this eternal world,—and thou mayest console thyself with the innumerable creatures that move and live and fade away with thee. But if this all,—with its smallest and its greatest creatures, with its wisdom and its might, with the wonder of its existence and the existence of its wonders,—is the work of a Being before whom thy soul need not tremble, before whom thou canst bow in the feeling of thy weakness and nothingness, and to whom thou canst look up, trusting in His love and compassion,—if thou dost feel truly that in thee lives something more lasting and eternal than the tissues of the flowers, the spheres of the planets, and the life of the beetle,—if thou dost recognise in thyself, as in a shadow, the lustre of the Eternal shining around thee,—if thou dost feel in thee and beneath thee and over thee the omnipresence of Him in whom thy semblance becomes being, thy agony rest, thy loneliness communion,—then thou knowest to whom thou dost cry in the darkest night of life, "Father, Thy will be done: as in heaven, so on earth; as on earth, so in me."

Then all within and around thee becomes clear: the morning twilight with its cold mists vanishes, and new warmth streams through trembling nature. Thou hast found a hand which thou wilt never leave,—which will hold thee when the mountains tremble and the planets are extinguished. Wherever thou art, thou art with Him, and He with Thee; He is the Ever-near; His is the world, with its flowers and thorns; and His is man, with his joys and sorrows. "Not the slightest thing can happen to thee,.but by the will of God."

With such thoughts I pursued my way, sometimes happy, sometimes sad; for even when we have attained rest and peace in the deepest recesses of the soul, it is difficult to remain in that holy solitude. Yes: many forget it again, after they have found it, and hardly know the way that will lead them back to it.

Weeks had flown by, and not a syllable from her had reached me. "Perhaps she is dead, and lies in quiet rest," was another song that floated on my tongue, and always returned as often as I drove it from me. It was possible; for the doctor had told me she had a heart complaint, and each morning when he went to her he was prepared to find her no longer alive. And if she had left this earth without my having taken leave of her, without my having told her even at the last moment how I loved her, could I ever forgive myself? Must I not follow her till I found her again, till I heard from her that she loved me, and that she forgave me? How men play with life, and delay from day to day the deed that they might do, and the greatest delight that they might enjoy, without thinking that every day, every hour may be their last, and that lost time is lost eternity!

Then all the words of the doctor, when I last saw him came back to me, and I felt that I had only resolved on my sudden departure to show him my firmness,—that it would have been harder to me to confess my weakness to him and remain. Now it seemed clear to me that there was but one duty for me,—to return to her without delay, and to bear all that Heaven might send us. But just as I had made a plan for my return, there suddenly rose to my memory the words of the old doctor: "As soon as possible she must go away into the country." She had herself told me that she generally spent the summer at her castle. Perhaps she was there, close to me; in a day I could be with her. No sooner thought than done. By day-break I had started, and in the evening I stood at the door of the castle.

The evening was still and bright. The summits

of the mountains shone in the full glory of a golden sunset, and the lower slopes were bathed in a rosy blue. From the valleys a grey mist was rising, which suddenly became bright when it floated up into the higher regions, and then like a sea of clouds floated towards heaven. And this whole play of colours was reflected again in the slightly heaving bosom of the dark lake, on whose shores the mountains seemed to rise and to sink; so that only the tops of the trees, and the pointed church tower, and the rising smoke from the houses, indicated the line where the real world parted from its reflection. But my eye was directed to one point only,—that was the old castle, where a presentiment told me I should find her again. No light was visible in the windows, no step broke the silence of evening. Had my presentiment deceived me? I went slowly through the first gateway, and up the steps, till

I stood in the court-yard of the castle. Here I saw a sentinel walking up and down, and I flew to him to inquire who was in the castle. " The Countess is here and her attendants," was the short answer; and in an instant I stood at the chief entrance and had already rung the bell. Then it first struck me what I had done. No one knew me, and I could not, dared not, say who I was. I had wandered for weeks through the mountains and looked like a beggar. What should I say? Whom should I ask for? But there was no time to consider. The door opened, and a porter in the princely livery stood before me, and looked wonderingly at me.

I asked whether the English lady, who I knew never left the Countess, was in the castle; and as the porter answered in the affirmative, I asked for paper and ink, and wrote to her that I was here to inquire how the Countess was.

H

The porter called a servant, who carried the letter upstairs. I heard each step in the long passages; and with each minute that I waited my position became more intolerable. On the walls hung old family pictures of the princely house: knights in full armour, ladies in old-fashioned costumes, and in the midst of them a woman in the white dress of a nun, with a red cross on her breast. At other times I had often seen these pictures and never thought how a human heart had once beat in every one of them. But now it seemed as if I could suddenly read whole volumes in their features, and as if they all said to me, " We too once lived, we too once suffered." Under this iron armour there once lay secrets concealed, as now in my heart. This white dress and this red cross are living witnesses that here too a struggle was fought, such as raged now in my breast. And then they all seemed to look on me with pity; then again a haughty pride lay in their features, as if they would say, " You do not belong to us." Every minute I became more restless, when suddenly a light step roused me from my dreams. The English lady came down the staircase and begged me to go into a room. I looked inquiringly at her, to see if she guessed what was going on. But every feature was perfectly unmoved, and without allowing herself the slightest expression of interest or surprise, she told me in a measured voice, that the Countess was much better to-day, and invited me to come to her in half-an-hour.

Like a good swimmer who ventures far out into the sea, and first thinks of his return when his arms begin to be tired, and then divides the waves with speed, and hardly dares to raise his eyes to the distant shore, who feels with every stroke that his power is failing, and yet will not own it, till at last, powerless and convulsed, he hardly preserves any consciousness of his situation,—then suddenly his feet touch the firm ground, and his arm grasps the first boulder of the shore,—so it was with me when I heard these words. A new life of reality approached me, and all I had suffered was a dream. There are but few such moments in a man's life, and thousands have never felt their magic. But the mother who for the first time cradles her child in her arms,—the father who receives back his only son from the war crowned with glory,—the poet whose own nation greets him with acclamations, the youth whose warm pressure of the hand is returned by some loved one with one yet warmer,—they know what is meant by a dream turned to reality.

The half-hour was over, and a servant came

and led me through a long suite of rooms, opened a door, and in the faint evening light I saw a white form, and above her a high window that looked over the lake and the gleaming mountains.

"How strangely people meet!" echoed her clear voice towards me, and each word was as a cool rain-drop after a hot summer's day.

"How strangely people meet, and how strangely they lose themselves!" I said, and seized her hand and felt that we were again by and with each other.

"But that is their own fault, when they lose themselves," she continued, and her voice, which always seemed to accompany her words like music, changed involuntarily into a minor key.

"Yes: that is true," I answered. "But tell me first, are you well? May I speak to you?"

"My dear friend," she said, smiling, "I am never well, as you know, and if I say that I feel well, I do so only for love of my old doctor, for he is quite certain that from my earliest years I owe my whole life to him only and to his skill. Before I left the capital I gave him a great fright, for one evening my heart suddenly ceased to beat, and I felt such agony that I thought it would never begin to beat again. But that is past, and why should we speak of it? Only one thing pains me. I always thought I should close my eyes in perfect quiet, but now I feel that my sufferings will disturb and embitter even my departure from life." Then she laid her hand on her heart, and said, "But tell me where you have been, and why, all this time I have heard nothing from you. The old doctor gave me so many reasons for your sudden journey that I at last said that I did not believe him, and then he gave me at length the most unbelievable of all reasons. Guess what?"

"It might appear incredible," I broke in, that she might not utter the word: "and yet perhaps it was but too true. But that too is past, and why should we speak of it?"

"But no, my friend," she said, "why should it be past? I told the doctor when he gave me the last reason for your sudden journey, that I understood neither him nor you. I am a poor, weak, lonely being, and my earthly existence is but a slow death. If heaven has sent me two souls who understand me, or, as the doctor expressed it, loved me, why should this disturb mine or their peace? I had just been reading in my favourite poet, old Wordsworth, when the doctor made his confesssion to me, and I said, 'My dear doctor, we have so many thoughts and so few words, that we are forced to mix together many thoughts in the same word.' If now any one who did not know us heard that my young friend loved me and I him, he might think it was as Romeo loved Juliet, and Juliet Romeo, and then you would be quite right in saying that must not be. But is it not true, my old doctor, that you also love me and I love you? and I have loved you for many years, and yet perhaps have never owned it to you yet. I am neither in despair nor unhappy from it. Yes, my dear doctor, I will say something more to you: I think you have a deep affection for me, and are jealous of our young friend. Do you not come every morning to see how I am, even when you know perfectly that I am quite well? Do you not bring me the finest flowers from your garden? Have I not been obliged to give you my picture?—and, I ought perhaps not to betray it,—did you not last Sunday come into my room, and you thought I was asleep? I really slept, or at least I could not have roused myself; but I saw you sitting a long time by my bed, your eyes immovably fixed on me, and I felt them like sunbeams playing on my face; and at last your eyes grew dim, and I felt great tears fall from them; then you hid your face in your hands and sobbed aloud, "Maria, Maria." Ah, my dear doctor, our young friend has never done that, and yet you have sent him away.' As I spoke so to him, half in fun, half in earnest, as I always speak, I felt I had hurt the old man; he became quite still and blushed like a child. Then I took a volume of Wordsworth's poems, in which I had just been reading, and said, 'Here is another old man whom I love with all my heart, who understands me and whom I understand, and yet I have never seen him and shall never see him,—that is the way of this world. Now I will read you a poem of his; then you will see how men can love, and how love is a quiet blessing which the lover lays on the head of the loved one, and then goes on his way in peaceful gladness.' Then I read him Wordsworth's 'Highland Girl.' And now, my friend, draw the lamp nearer and read me that poem again, for it refreshes me whenever I hear it; a spirit breathes in it like the quiet infinite glow of evening that yonder lovingly spreads its arms in blessing round the pure breast of the snow-clad mountains."

As her words sounded slowly and quietly through my soul, all within my breast became again still and solemn. The storm was over, and her image floated like the silver image of the moon on the gently-stirred waves of my love, —this universal sea, which streams through the hearts of all men, and that every one calls his own, whilst it is really the pulse that animates all humanity. I would rather have been silent like nature, which lay stretched there before our eyes, and which became ever stiller and darker; but she gave me the book, and so I read :—

"Sweet Highland girl, a very shower
Of beauty is thy earthly dower!
Twice seven consenting years have shed
Their utmost bounty on thy head;
And these grey rocks; that household lawn;
Those trees, a veil just half withdrawn;
This fall of water that doth make
A murmur near the silent lake;
This little bay; a quiet road
That holds in shelter thy abode,—
In truth together do ye seem
Like something fashioned in a dream:
Such forms as from their covert peep
When earthly cares are laid asleep!
But, O fair creature! in the light
Of common day, so heavenly bright,
I bless thee, vision as thou art,
I bless thee with a human heart:
God shield thee to thy latest years!
Thee neither know I, nor thy peers,

And yet my eyes are filled with tears.
   With earnest feeling I shall pray
For thee when I am far away;
For never saw I mien or face
In which more plainly I could trace
Benignity and homebred sense
Ripening in perfect innocence.
Here scattered, like a random seed,
Remote from men, thou dost not need
The embarrassed look of shy distress
And maidenly shamefacedness;
Thou wear'st upon thy forehead clear
The freedom of a mountaineer;
A face with gladness overspread!
Soft smiles, by human kindness bred!
And seemliness complete, that sways
Thy courtesies, about thee plays
With no restraint, but such as springs
From quick and eager visitings
Of thoughts that lie beyond the reach
Of thy few words of English speech:
A bondage sweetly brook'd, a strife
That gives thy gestures grace and life!
So have I, not unmoved in mind,
Seen birds of tempest-loving kind
Thus beating up against the wind.

What hand but would a garland cull
For thee who art so beautiful?
O happy pleasure! here to dwell
Beside thee in some heathy dell;
Adopt your homely ways and dress,
A shepherd, thou a shepherdess!
But I could frame a wish for thee
More like a grave reality:
Thou art to me but as a wave
Of the wild sea; and I would have
Some claim upon thee, if I could,
Though but of common neighbourhood.
What joy to hear thee, and to see!
Thy elder brother I would be,
Thy father,—anything to thee!

Now, thanks to Heaven! that of its grace
Hath led me to this lonely place.
Joy have I had; and going hence
I bear away my recompense.
In spots like these it is we prize
Our memory,—feel that she hath eyes·
Then why should I be loth to stir?
I feel this place was made for her,
To give new pleasure like the past,
Continued long as life shall last.
Nor am I loth, though pleased at heart,

> Sweet Highland girl! from thee to part;
> For I, methinks, till I grow old,
> As fair before me shall behold,
> As I do now, the cabin small,
> The lake, the bay, the waterfall,
> And thee, the spirit of them all!"

I had ended, and the poem had been to me as a draught of fresh spring water, such as I had lately so often drunk out of the cup of some great green leaf.

Then I heard her soft voice, like the first notes of an organ which rouse us from our dreaming prayer, and she said: "So I wish you to love me, and so the old doctor loves me, and so in one way or another we ought all of us to love and believe in each other. But the world, although I know it so little, seems not to understand this love and faith, and men have made of this earth, where we might have lived so happily, a sad desert. It must have been different in early times, or how could Homer have created the lovable, healthy, tender form of Nausicaa. Nausicaa loved Odysseus at first sight. She says so at once, to her friends: 'Oh, that such a man might be called my husband! that he would be content to remain here!' But yet she is ashamed to appear with him at once in the city, and she tells him openly that if she took home with her so handsome and stately a stranger the people would say she had been to fetch a husband. How simple and natural is all this. But when she hears that he wishes to return home to his wife and child, no murmur escapes her: she disappears from our sight, and we feel that she long carried in her heart the image of the handsome, stately stranger, in silent, joyful admiration. Why do not our poets know this love, this happy confession, this quiet parting? A modern poet would have made

Nausicaa into a female Werther, and that is because love is nothing more for us than a prelude to the comedy or tragedy of marriage. Is there, then, really no other love now? Is the source of this pure happiness quite dried up? Do men only know the intoxicating drink, and not the refreshing spring of love?"

At these words I thought of the English poet who complains:—

> " From heaven if this belief be sent,
> If such be nature's holy plan,
> Have I not reason to lament
> What man has made of man?"

"But how happy are the poets," she said; "their words call the deepest feelings of a thousand dumb hearts into life, and how often have their songs been used as the confession of the sweetest secrets! Their heart beats in the breasts of the poor and the rich; the fortunate sing and the afflicted weep with them. But there is no poet I can so entirely feel my own as Wordsworth. I know many of my friends do not love him; they say he is no poet: but it is just this that I love in him. He avoids all ordinary poet's phrases, all exaggeration, and all that one means by the expression 'poetical flights.' He is *true;* and does not everything lie in this word? He opens our eyes to the beauty that, like the daisy in the meadows, lies beneath our feet; he calls everything by its real name; he will not surprise, deceive, or dazzle; he will only show men how beautiful all is that is not yet distorted and destroyed by the hand of man. Is not a dew-drop on a blade of grass more beautiful than a pearl set in gold? Is not a living spring that trickles towards us we know not whence, more wonderful than all the fountains of Versailles? Is not his 'Highland Girl' more lovable and a truer expression of real beauty than Goethe's 'Helena,' or Byron's 'Haydee?' And then the simplicity of his language, the purity of his thoughts! What a pity that we have never had such a poet! Schiller might have been our Wordsworth had he trusted more in himself than in the old Greeks and Romans. Our Rückert comes the nearest to him, if he had not sought for comfort and home away from his own poor fatherland, among Eastern roses. Few poets have courage to be exactly *that* which they are. Wordsworth had it; and as we willingly listen to great men even when they are not great, but, like other mortals, quietly cherish their thoughts and wait in patience for the moment when a clear gleam may open to them fresh visions of the infinite, so I like Wordsworth even in those poems which contain nothing but what every one could have said. Great poets give themselves rest; in Homer we often read a hundred verses without one single beauty, and so in Dante; whilst Pindar, whom you all admire so, drives me to despair by his ecstacies. What would I not give to be able to pass a summer at the lakes, and visit with Wordsworth all the places to which he has given names, and greet all the trees he has saved from the axe, and watch with him, for once, the distant sunset, which he described as only Turner could have painted it!"

It was remarkable how her voice never sank, as with most people, at the end of her sentences, but, on the contrary, rose, and always ended like an interrogative leading note! She always spoke up, not down, to people. The melody of her sentences was as when a child says, "Is it not so, Father?" There was something imploring in her tone, and it was almost impossible to contradict her.

"Wordsworth," I said, "is dear to me as poet, still dearer as a man: and as we often have a finer, fuller, more life-like view from a small hill that we ascend without fatigue, than if with difficulty and danger we clambered up Mont Blanc, so I feel it is with Wordsworth's poetry. At first it often appeared common-place to me, and I have often laid down his poems, and could not imagine how the best minds of modern England could cherish such admiration for him. But I have convinced myself that no poet in any language, who is recognised as a true poet by his own nation, or rather by the noblest minds among his own people, should remain unenjoyed by us. Admiration is an art that we must learn. Many Germans say, Racine does not please us; an Englishman says, I cannot understand Goethe; the Frenchman says, Shakespeare is a clown. And what does that mean? Nothing more than if a child says he prefers a Valse to one of Beethoven's Symphonies. The real art is to discover and understand what each nation admires in its great men, and he who seeks the beautiful will at length find it, and perceive that even the Persians are not entirely deceived in their Hafis, nor the Hindus in their Kâlidâsa. One does not understand a great man at once, it requires strength, courage, and perseverance; and it is remarkable that what pleases us at first sight, seldom captivates us for long."

"And yet," she said, "there is one thing that is common to all great poets, all true artists, all heroes on earth, be they Persians or Hindus, heathens or Christians, Romans or Germans; that is,—I hardly know how to express it,—but it is the Infinite which seems to lie behind them; a clear sight into the Eternal, an apotheosis of everything, even the smallest, the most transient.

Goethe, the great Pagan, knows the sweet 'peace that is from heaven'; and when he sings—

> 'On every hill is quiet now,
>   Among the tree-tops tracest thou
>   Scarcely a breath.
>   The small birds sleep among the trees;
>   Wait, only wait, and soon like these,
>   Thou too shalt rest,'—*

does there not open above the summits of the lofty pine trees, an endless space, a rest which earth can never give? This background is never wanting in Wordsworth, and the scoffers may say what they like, but it is only that which is above the earth, be it ever so concealed, that can stir, and move the human heart. Who under-

---

* Ueber allen Gipfeln
Ist Ruh;
In allen Wipfeln
Spürest du
Kaum einen Hauch;
Die Vöglein schweigen im Walde;
Warte nur, balde,
Ruhest du auch.

stood earthly beauty better than Michael Angelo? but he understood it because it was to him a reflection of celestial beauty. You know his sonnet—

  'Rapt above earth by power of one fair face,—
    Hers in whose sway alone my heart delights,—
    I mingle with the blest, on those pure heights
    Where man, yet mortal, rarely finds a place.
    With Him who made the work that work accords
    So well, that by its help and through His grace
    I raise my thoughts, inform my deeds and words,
    Clasping her beauty in my soul's embrace.
    Thus, if from two fair eyes mine cannot turn,
    I feel how in their presence doth abide
    Light, which to God is both the way and guide;
    And kindling at their lustre, if I burn,
    My noble fire emits the joyful ray
    That through the realms of glory shines for aye.'"*

                  Wordsworth's Translation.

---

    * La forza d'un bel volto al ciel mi sprona
      (Ch'altro in terra non è che mi diletti),
      E vivo ascendo tra gli spirti eletti;
      Grazia ch'ad uom mortal raro si dona.

She was exhausted and ceased speaking ; and how could I have disturbed that silence ? When, after an intimate exchange of thoughts, human hearts feel satisfied and are silent, we say well that an angel flies through the room ; and it seemed to me that I could hear the light wings of the angel of peace and love above our heads. Whilst my eye rested on her, her earthly vesture seemed as though transfigured in the twilight of the summer evening, and only her hand, which I held in mine, assured me of her real presence. Then a bright ray of light fell suddenly on her face, and she felt it, opened her eyes and looked

> Si ben col suo Fattor l'opra consuona.
> Ch'a lui mi levo per divin concetti.
> E quivi informo i pensier tutti e i detti ;
> Ardendo, amando per gentil persona.
>
> Onde, se mai da due begli occhi il guardo
> Torcer non so, conosco in lor la luce
> Che mi mostra la via, ch'a Dio mi guide ;
> E se nel lume loro acceso io ardo,
> Nel nobil foco mio dolce riluce
> La gioja che nel cielo eterna ride.

at me as if astonished. Her wonderfully lustrous eyes, which the half-closed eyelashes covered like a veil, flashed like lightning. I looked round and at length saw how the moon had risen in her full beauty between two mountains opposite the castle, and shed its friendly smile over the lake and village. Never had I seen nature—never had I seen her dear face—so beautiful; never had such a blessed calm flowed over my soul. "Maria," I said, "let me, such as I am, in this rapturous moment confess my whole love to you. Now, when we feel so intensely the nearness of the unearthly, let us unite our souls in a bond that nothing on earth may again divide. Whatever love is, Maria, I love you; and I feel, Maria, you are mine, for I am yours."

I knelt before her, and dared not look into her eyes. My lips touched her hand, and I kissed it. Then she drew away her hand, first slowly, then hastily and decidedly; and when I looked up I saw an expression of pain in her face. She was still silent, at last she raised herself with a deep sigh and said:—

"Enough for to-day: you have hurt me; but it is my fault. Close the window: I feel a cold shudder over me, as if a strange hand were touching me. Stay with me,—yet no; you must go. Farewell, sleep well,—and pray that the peace of God may abide with us. We shall meet again, shall we not, to-morrow evening? I shall expect you."

Oh, where had all that heavenly rest flown in a moment? I saw how she suffered, and all I could do was to hasten out and call the English lady, and go alone to the village in the darkness of night. Long I walked beside the lake; long my eyes strayed towards the lighted window, where I had just been with her. At length every light in the Castle was extinguished, the moon rose higher and higher, and each point and balcony and ornament of the old walls became visible in the fairy-like illumination. And here was I alone in the silent night, and my brain seemed to refuse to obey me, for no thought came to any conclusion, and I only felt that I was solitary in the world; that there was no soul for me. The earth was like a coffin, and the dark heavens like a winding-sheet, and I scarcely knew whether I was still alive, or had long been dead. Then I suddenly looked up to the stars, with their twinkling eyes pursuing their course so quietly; and they seemed as if only placed there to lighten and comfort mankind; and I thought of two heavenly stars that had risen on my dark horizon, and a thanksgiving rose from my breast, a thanksgiving for the love of my good angel.

LAST RECOLLECTION.

THE sun was shining over the mountains and into my window when I awoke. Was it the same sun that had watched us yesterday evening with a long lingering look, like a parting friend, as if it would bless the union of our souls, and that then sank like a vanished hope! And now it shone on me, like a child that rushes into our room with a bright face to wish us joy of some happy festival. And was I the same being who but a few hours before had thrown himself on his bed, broken in spirit and in body! And now I felt again the old energy rising in me, and a trust in God and myself, that refreshed and animated my soul like the cool morning breeze.

What would become of man without sleep? We know not whither this nightly messenger leads us; and when he closes our eyes of an evening, who will give us a pledge that he will open them again for us in the morning, and restore us to ourselves? It required courage and faith when the first man sank into the arms of this unknown friend; and were there not something helpless in our nature, that forces us to have faith in everything which we are meant to believe, and constrains us to submit, I doubt whether any man, in spite of all fatigue, would have closed his eyes of his own free-will, to enter that unknown dreamland. The sense of our weakness and weariness gives us trust in a higher power, and courage to resign ourselves gladly to the beautiful ordering of all things;

ay, we feel strengthened and refreshed when we have loosened, if only for a short time, either waking or sleeping, the chains that fasten down our eternal to our earthly Self.

What had yesterday only passed darkly through my mind like an evening mist, was now instantly clear. I felt that we belonged to each other, be it as brother and sister, as parent and child, as bridegroom and bride,—that we must now and for ever remain undivided. It was only needful to find the right name for that which in our stammering language we call love.

> "Thy elder brother I would be,
> Thy father—anything to thee."

It was this *anything* for which a name must be found; for the world, once for all, will acknowledge nothing without a name. She had herself said that she loved me with that pure love for all mankind, out of which springs all other love. Her fear, her displeasure, when I confessed my full love to her were still unintelligible to me, but they could no longer shake my belief in our mutual affection. Why should we try to understand all that passes in the souls of men, when everything in ourselves is so incomprehensible? It is always the inexplicable that mostly captivates us, be it in nature, in men, or in our own breast. People whom we understand, and whose motives we see before us like an anatomical preparation, leave us cold, like the characters in most of our novels; and nothing destroys our delight in life and mankind more than this ethical rationalism, which would explain everything, and denies all miracles in the soul. There is in every being something that cannot be analysed, call it fate, inspiration, or character; and he neither knows himself nor mankind who believes that he can examine the deeds and efforts of men, without finding this ever-returning residuum. So I took heart about everything that I had despaired of over-night, till at length not a cloud was left to darken the bright sky of my future.

In this mind I stepped out of the small house into the open air, when a messenger brought me a letter. It was from the Countess; that I could tell from the beautiful even writing. I opened it breathlessly: I hoped the dearest that man can hope. But soon all my hopes were crushed. The letter contained nothing but a request not to see her to-day, as she expected visitors at the castle. No friendly word; no news of her health: only at the end a P.S.—"To-morrow comes the Doctor. So the day after to-morrow."

Here were at once two days torn out of the book of life! If they had but been quite torn out: but no, they hung over my head like the leaden roof of a prison. They must be lived through: I could not give them as an alms to a king or a beggar, who would gladly have had two more days to sit on his throne, or on his seat by the church door. I stood staring blankly for a long time, and then I thought of my morning prayer, and how I had said to myself that there is no greater want of faith than despair, and how the least and the greatest events in life are part of one great Divine plan, to which we must submit ourselves, however difficult it may be. Like a rider who sees an abyss before him I drew in my reins. "Let it be since. it must," I cried to myself: "but God's earth is not the place for lamentations and grief." Was it not bliss to hold in my hand these lines which she had written, and was not the hope of seeing her again soon a greater blessing than I ever deserved? Always keep your head above the waves, every good swimmer through life will tell you; but if you can no longer do so, it is better to plunge under entirely than to let the water keep running into your eyes and throat. And if it is difficult always to remember Divine providence in the little misfortunes of life, and if we hesitate, and perhaps rightly, to step out of the ordinary course of life into the presence of the Deity at every struggle, yet life should appear to us, if not as a duty, yet as an art;—and what is more ugly than a child that flies into a passion or sulks at every disappointment and pain? Nothing is more beautiful than a child in whose tearful eyes the sunshine of joy and innocence is already sparkling again, like a flower which trembles and bends under an April shower, but soon blooms and sends forth its scent, whilst the sunshine dries the tear-drops from off its cheeks.

Soon a good idea occurred to me, of how, in spite of my fate, I might still pass these two days with her. I had long wished to record all the dear words that she had spoken to me and the many beautiful thoughts which she had entrusted to me; and so the days passed in the recollection of precious hours spent together, and in the hope of a yet fairer future. I was near her and with her and living in her, and felt the nearness of her spirit and her love more than I had ever felt them when her hand lay in mine.

How dear are these pages to me now! How often I have read and re-read them; not as though I had forgotten a word which she said to me; but these papers are the proofs of my happiness, and something looks out of them at me like the face of a friend whose silence says more than all words. Recollections of past happiness, of past sorrow, a silent sinking into a distant past, where all disappears that now surrounds and oppresses us, where the soul casts itself down like a mother on the green grave of her child who has slept there for many years, where no hope, no wish disturbs the stillness of helpless resignation,—this we indeed call sadness: but there is a blessedness in such sadness known only to those who loved much and suffered much. Ask the mother what she feels when she fastens the veil, which she once wore as a bride, on her daughter's head, and thinks of her husband, no longer with her; ask the man what he feels when the young girl whom he loved, and whom the world parted from him, sends him back, after her death, the withered rose that he had given her as a youth. They may both weep, but the tears are not tears of sorrow nor tears of joy; they are the tears of sacrifice with which man dedicates himself to God, and quietly sees his most precious treasure pass away, believing in God's love and wisdom.

But let us return to our recollections, into the very presence of the past. The two days flew by so fast that a tremor of joy shot through me as the happiness of our meeting drew nearer and nearer. I saw how on the first day the carriages and riders arrived from the city, and the castle was alive with joyous guests. The flags waved from the roof, music sounded through the courts. In the evening the lake was covered with gay gondolas, bass voices sounded over the water, and I could not but listen, for I felt she was listening too at her window to the same songs. The second day all were still busy, but in the afternoon the guests prepared for their departure, and late in the evening I saw the carriage of the old doctor return alone towards the city. Then I could wait no longer. I knew she was alone; I knew she was thinking of me, and wishing that I was with her. Should I let another night go by without at least pressing her hand, without telling her that the separation was over, and that the next morning would wake us to new happiness? There was still a light in her window, and why should she be left there alone? Why should I not at least for a moment feel her sweet presence? I already stood at the castle, and would have rung the bell: then suddenly I stopped and said, "No; no weakness! You would stand ashamed before her, like a thief in the night. Early to-morrow go to her like a hero returning from the battle, for whom she now wreathes the crown of love to place on his head."

The morning came, and I was with her, really

with her. Oh, speak not of spirit as if it could exist without body! Perfect existence, perfect consciousness and joy can be only where spirit and body are one,—an embodied spirit, a spiritual body! There is no spirit without a body unless it be a ghost, and no body without a spirit unless it be a corpse. Is the flower of the field without a spirit? Does it not look forth through a Divine will, through a creative thought, which preserves it, and gives it life and existence? That is its spirit; only it is dumb in the flowers, whilst in man it reveals itself in words. True life is ever bodily and spiritual life—true enjoyment is ever bodily and spiritual enjoyment—true presence is ever presence in body and in spirit, and the whole world of recollections in which I had lived so happily for two days vanished like a shadow, like a thing of nought, when I stood before her, and was really with her. I should have liked to lay my hands on her forehead and eyes, and then to know, really know, that she was truly there, and not merely the image that floated day and night over my soul, but a being that was not mine, and yet was to be and wished to be mine—a being in whom I could believe as in myself, a being far from me, and yet nearer to me than my own self, a being without whom my life would be no life, even my death no death, without whom my poor existence would have been lost, like a sigh, in infinite space. I felt, as my looks and thoughts dwelt on her, that in this moment the bliss of my existence was accomplished, and a shudder ran through me, and I thought of death, but it appeared to have no longer any terrors for me, for death could not destroy *this* love, but could only purify, ennoble, and immortalize it.

It was so sweet to be silent with her. The full depth of her soul mirrored itself on her countenance; and as I looked at her I already saw and heard all that was living and hidden in her. "You give me pain," she seemed to say, and yet would not say it. "Are we at last together again? Be quiet; do not question; do not despair: you are welcome. Do not be angry with me." All this was expressed by her eyes, and yet she dared not destroy the peace of our happiness by a single word.

"Have you received a letter from the doctor?" was her first question, and her voice trembled at every word.

"No," I answered.

She was silent for a time, then said, "Perhaps it is better that it happened so, and that I should tell you all myself. My friend, we see each other to-day for the last time. Let us part in peace, without complaint. I have done you great wrong. I feel that I have laid hold on your life, without thinking how even a light breath will rob a flower of its petals. I know the world so little that I did not think a poor suffering being like me could inspire you with any deeper feeling than mere pity. I met you frankly and warmly because I had known you so long, because I felt so happy in your presence, because—why should I not confess the whole truth?—I loved you. But the world does not understand this love, nor allow it. The Doctor has opened my eyes. The whole city is talking of us. My brother, the Regent, has written to the Prince, and he requires me never to see you again. I deeply grieve that I have caused you this suffering: tell me that you forgive me, and then let us part as friends."

Her eyes were filled with tears, but she closed,

them, that I might not see it. "Maria," I said, "for me there is but one life, and that is with you; but also only one will, that is yours. Yes, I confess it: I love you with the full fervour of love; but I am not worthy of you. You are far above me in rank, in nobleness, in innocence, and I can hardly grasp the thought of ever calling you my wife; and yet there is no other way by which we can pass through life together. Maria, you are quite free: I ask no sacrifice. The world is wide, and if you wish it, we need never meet again. . But if you feel that you love me, if you feel you are mine, oh, then let us forget the world and its cold judgment! In my arms I will carry you to the altar, and kneeling, swear to be yours in life and death."

"My friend," she said, "we must never desire the impossible. Had it been God's will that such a bond should unite us in this life, would

He have sent me these sufferings, which make it impossible for me to be more than a helpless child? Do not forget that what we call fate, circumstance, and position in life, are in truth the work of Providence. To resist them is to resist God; and, were it not childish, one would call it wicked. Men wander here on earth like the stars in heaven. God has given them their course, where they meet each other, and when they ought to part, they must part. Their resistance would be useless, it would destroy the whole order of the universe. We cannot understand, but we can trust. I cannot myself understand why my affection for you is wrong. No: I cannot, will not call it wrong. But it cannot be, must not be. My friend, this is enough; we must submit in humility and faith."

Notwithstanding the calmness with which she spoke, I saw how deeply she suffered, and yet

I felt it would be wrong to give up so quickly the struggle for life. I controlled myself as far as I could, that no word of passion might increase her sufferings, and said,

"If this is the last time we are to meet in this life, let us clearly see to *whom* we offer this sacrifice. If our love violated a higher law, like you I would bow in humility. It would be forgetting God to oppose a higher will. It may sometimes seem as if man could deceive God,—as if his small sagacity might overreach the Divine wisdom. That is madness, and the man who began this Titan's conflict would be crushed and annihilated. But what opposes our love? Nothing but the gossip of the world. I honour the laws of human society,—honour them even when they are, as in our time, over-refined and perplexed. A diseased body requires artificial medicines; and without the barriers, and prejudices, and conventionalities of society, which we laugh at, it would be impossible to hold men together at the present day, and to attain the object for which we are placed here on earth. We must sacrifice much to these false gods, and, like the Athenians, we send every year a heavily laden ship of young men and maidens as a tribute to the monster who rules the labyrinth of our social existence. There is scarcely a heart that has not been broken,—there is hardly a man with true feeling who has not been obliged to clip the wings of his love, ere it would rest quietly in the cage of the modern world. It must be so; it cannot be otherwise. You do not know life; but if I only think of my friends, I could tell you whole volumes of tragedies. One loved a maiden, and was loved in return: but he was poor; she was rich. The parents and relations quarrelled and insulted each other: and two hearts were broken. Why? Because in this world it is thought a misfortune that a lady should wear a dress made from the wool of a plant in America, and not from the fibres of a worm in China.

"Another loved a maiden, and was loved in return: but he was a Protestant; she a Roman Catholic. The mothers and priests made mischief,—and two hearts were broken. Why? Because of the political game of chess played by Charles V., Francis I., and Henry VIII., three centuries ago.

"A third loved a maiden and was loved again: but he was noble; she was plebeian. The sisters were angry and jealous,—and two hearts were broken. Why? Because a hundred years ago a soldier slew another, who threatened a King's life in battle. His sovereign gave him rank and honour, and his great-grandson atones, with a blighted life, for the blood which then was shed.

"The collectors of statistics say that every hour a heart is broken,—and I believe it. And why? Because in most cases the world will acknowledge no love between strangers, unless they become man and wife. If two maidens love the same man, one must fall a sacrifice. If two men love the same woman, one or both must be sacrificed. Why? Can no one love a maiden without wishing to marry her? Can no one love a woman without trying to carry her off as his booty? You shut your eyes, and I feel I have said too much. The world has desecrated the holiest things we have in life. But enough, Maria! Let us use the language of the world when we are in it, and speak and act with it; but let us preserve one sanctuary in which two hearts may speak the pure language of the heart unmoved by the anger of the world without. The world itself honours this independent and courageous resistance, which noble hearts, conscious of their own rights, oppose to the ordinary course of things. The discretions, the proprieties, the prejudices of the world are like parasite-plants. It is beautiful when a fine ivy adorns a strong wall with its thousand tendrils and shoots, but it must not grow too luxuriously, else it penetrates into every corner of the edifice and destroys the cement which is to hold it together. Be mine, Maria! Follow the dictates of your heart. The word now trembling on your lips decides for ever your life and mine,—your happiness and mine."

I was silent. Her hand which I held, returned the warm heartfelt pressure. All within her was moved and shaken; and the blue sky which lay before me had never seemed so lovely as now when the storm drove across it cloud after cloud.

L

"And why do you love me?" she said; as if she must still delay the moment of decision.

"Why? Maria! Ask the child why it is born; ask the flower why it blooms; ask the sun why it shines! Love you? Because I must love you! But if I must say more to you, let this book which lies by you, and which you love so deeply, speak for me:—

"'That which is best should be the dearest of all things to us; and in our love of it, neither helpfulness nor unhelpfulness, advantage nor injury, gain nor loss, honour nor dishonour, praise nor blame, nor any thing of the kind should be regarded; but what is in truth the noblest and best of all things should be also the dearest of all things, and that for no other cause than that it is the noblest and best. Hereby may a man order his life within and without. His outward life, for among the creatures one is better than another, according as the Eternal Good manifesteth itself and worketh more in one than in another. Now that creature in which the Eternal Good most manifesteth itself, shineth forth, worketh, is most known and loved, is the best' and that wherein the Eternal Good is the least manifested is the least good of all creatures. Therefore when we have to do with the creatures, and hold converse with them, and take note of this distinction, the best creatures must always be the dearest to us, and we must cleave to them, and unite ourselves with them.'

"Maria, because you are the best creature I know, therefore I love you, and you are dear to me:—therefore we love each other. Say the word that is living in you,—say that you are mine; do not be false to your deepest feelings. God has sent you a suffering life,—He sends me to you to suffer with you. Your suffering shall be my suffering, and we will bear it together, as a ship carries the heavy sails that at length take it safely through the storms of life into a secure harbour."

She became more and more calm. A light flush played on her cheeks, like the quiet glow of evening. Then she opened her eyes wide, and the sun shone out once again with wonderful brilliancy.

"I am yours," she said: "God wills it. Take me as I am: so long as I live I am yours, and may God re-unite us in a brighter life and reward you for your love."

We lay heart to heart, my lips closed with a light kiss those lips on which the blessing of my life had just trembled. Time stood still for us,—the world around us vanished. At last she heaved a deep sigh. "May God forgive me this happiness," she whispered. "Now leave me alone! I can bear it no longer. May we meet again, my friend, my beloved, my bliss."

* * * * *

These were the last words I heard from her. Yet no. I went home and lay on my bed in anxious dreams. It was past midnight when the old Doctor entered my room. "Our angel is in heaven," he said: "here is the last greeting she sends you." With these words he gave me a letter. It contained the ring that she had once given to me and I to her again, with the words, "As God wills." It was wrapped in a worn paper, on which she had at some time written the words that I said to her as a child,—"What is yours is mine. Your Maria."

For hours we sat together without saying a word. It was a mental swoon, such as heaven sends us when the burden of sorrow is too heavy for us to bear. At last the old man rose, took my hand, and said, "We see each other to-day for the last time, for you must away from here and my days are numbered. There is one thing I must tell you : it is a secret which I have carried within me my whole life long and confessed it to no one. But I must tell it to some one now. Listen to me. The soul that is gone from us was a lovely soul—a noble, pure spirit—a deep, true heart. I knew a soul as fair as hers, still fairer, it was her mother's. I loved her mother and her mother loved me. We were both poor, and I struggled with life to win an honourable position in the world for her and me. The young Prince saw her and loved her. He was my Prince, and loved her truly, and was ready to sacrifice everything for her, and raise her, the poor orphan, to the rank of Princess. I loved her so that I sacrificed my happiness to my affection for her. I left my home and wrote to her that I released her from all engagements. I never saw her again till on her death-bed. She died at the birth of her daughter. Now you know why I loved your Maria and tried to prolong her life from day to day. She was the only being that still bound my heart to this earth. Bear life as I have borne it: waste not a day in idle sorrow. Help men wherever you can, love them, and thank God that you have seen upon earth such a heart as hers, have known, have loved, and—lost it."

"As God wills," I said, and we parted for life.

* * * * *

And days, and weeks, and months, and years have passed by. My native land has become strange to me, and the land of the stranger has become my home. But her love has remained to me, and as a tear falls into the sea, so has my love to her fallen into the living sea of humanity, penetrating and embracing millions—millions of those strangers whom I have loved so well from my childhood.

* * * * *

Only on still summer days, like to-day, when I lie alone in the green forest on the bosom of nature, and know not whether beyond its circles there are any other men, or whether I am alone, quite alone on the earth, then there is a movement in the churchyard of memory, old recollections rise up from their graves, and the full omnipotence of love returns back into the heart, and streams forth again towards that fair being who once more gazes on me with her deep unfathomable eyes; and then my love for all seems to vanish in my love for the one,—for my good angel; and my thoughts are dumb before the inscrutable mystery of finite and infinite love.

THE END.

www.ingramcontent.com/pod-product-compliance
Lightning Source LLC
Chambersburg PA
CBHW030307170426
43202CB00009B/908